ESSENTIAL TIPS

Everyday

MEDITATION

ESSENTIAL 101 TIPS

Everyday

MEDITATION

Naomi Ozaniec

DORLING KINDERSLEY
London • New York • Sydney • Moscow

A DORLING KINDERSLEY BOOK

Editor Clare Double
Art Editor Martin Hendry
Senior Editor Gillian Roberts
Series Art Editor Alison Donovan
Production Controller Hélène Lamassoure

First published in Great Britain in 1997 by
Dorling Kindersley Limited,
9 Henrietta Street, London WC2E 8PS

Visit us on the World Wide Web at http://www.dk.com

A CIP catalogue record for this book is available from the British Library

ISBN 0-7513-0479-4

Text film output by The Right Type, Great Britain
Reproduced by Colourscan, Singapore
Printed and bound by Graphicom, Italy

ESSENTIAL TIPS

WHY MEDITATE?

1 WHAT IS MEDITATION?

This ancient discipline involves contemplation while focusing your mind on a thought or object. It is a practice that can enable you to understand everything in your life more clearly. Meditation helps you examine what is happening to yourself as a whole person. It is a way of getting to know yourself that can transform and reveal your life in a new perspective.

2 MEDITATION & RELIGION

Meditative practices are part of many religious traditions. There are several common principles: outwardly, an awareness of posture, breath, and mental control; inwardly, a spiritual search. Buddhism is best known for its teaching on meditation, and takes various forms, including Zen. The Islamic Sufi Way, Judaism, Christian mysticism, and many Paths of Yoga also include meditative practices.

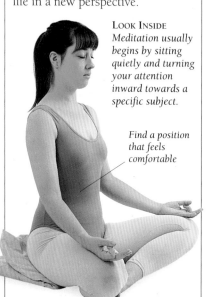

LOOK INSIDE
Meditation usually begins by sitting quietly and turning your attention inward towards a specific subject.

Find a position that feels comfortable

TRADITIONAL MEDITATION
India is home to a number of living spiritual traditions. It is still common to find a holy man like this one seated deep in meditation by a roadside shrine.

◁ TIBETAN THOUGHT
This section of a Tibetan lama's ritual headdress shows one of the five Buddhas of Meditation. This buddha embodies perfect knowledge.

Each buddha lives in a heavenly world

Vairochana, the foremost buddha

▽ PEACEFUL LIFE
A boy monk sits reading in a temple in north Thailand. Meditation is central to Buddhist monks' way of life and teaching.

◁ BOOK OF KELLS
Christian monks illuminated religious manuscripts like the Book of Kells during their lives of devotion and contemplation.

AWAKENED ONE
The Buddha got this name gaining enlightenment as he meditated under a Bo tree.

3 ANSWERS TO QUESTIONS

- You can start learning on your own. Later you might want to join a group or organization.
- You don't have to be religious to learn to meditate; just start from wherever you are now.
- A meditative state has nothing in common with being in a trance.
- There are teachers in many countries, not just in the East.
- Yes, meditation will change you.

ACTIVE MEDITATION
These Mevlevi Sufis, sometimes called whirling dervishes, spin (like the earth's axis) while in a state of deep meditation.

4 AIMS & INTENTIONS

Through meditation, you will aim to develop a deeper understanding of who you are and who you may become. With time, you will discover where your true nature and abilities lie. You will develop awareness – the capacity to notice fully every event in your life as it happens. Meditation brings an expansion of awareness in heart and mind that will make your life richer and more fulfilled.

△ **GLOBAL PERSPECTIVE**
Seeing earth from space may be the basis for a meditation. Develop your own ideals and values; see where you fit in.

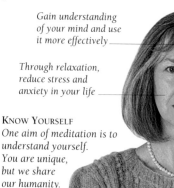

Gain understanding of your mind and use it more effectively

Through relaxation, reduce stress and anxiety in your life

KNOW YOURSELF
One aim of meditation is to understand yourself. You are unique, but we share our humanity.

BROADEN YOUR HORIZONS
Meditation will inspire you to find your own creativity and inner resources. You may feel encouraged to get the most benefit out of each day.

5 PHYSICAL & MENTAL BENEFITS

Meditation will benefit you as a whole person. It promotes physical relaxation and calm. A relaxed state is good for your heart and pulse rate, and your new awareness of breathing and posture will bring increased energy. In meditation, your brain waves are in a different state from those of either waking or sleeping, and both sides of your brain are active. Meditation unites mind and body. You can find peace of mind by learning to detach yourself from troubling thoughts. Your powers of concentration will sharpen with practice, too.

◁ USE YOUR TALENTS
Music is a rich field for creativity and enjoyment. Listen with awareness to discover its qualities.

△ EASE OF MIND
A full and active life with less stress and anxiety promotes restful and refreshing sleep.

Make the most of every opportunity, however small: read and relax

You will feel more energetic and able to cope with life

6 TAKING STOCK

Spend time taking stock of yourself and the values by which you live. Begin by examining your life as it is today. Reflect honestly on the life that you have created. Have you developed your real interests? Does your lifestyle nourish your health? Do you work too hard? Discover what your priorities are. Taking stock is like sorting out your wardrobe. Decide what you really want to keep and what is now worn out.

FORMATIVE INFLUENCES
Review what is important to you. List your values, not those of family and friends.

7 MAP YOUR JOURNEY

WHICH WAY NOW?

Life is often likened to a journey. Use this idea to look more closely at your life. Draw a map, any way you like, showing your travels so far. Put in important landmarks such as friends, family, and major events. Has your journey been an uphill climb or plain sailing? Your life map will help you to realize where you want to be in life.

UNCOVER YOUR TRACKS
We all leave footprints in the past. Don't be afraid to look at them. It is important to look back if you want to acknowledge where you have come to be in life.

8 LAUNCHING OUT

Once you have spent time taking stock of your life, you may feel ready to start learning how to meditate. Now you have mapped your journey, you can leave the past and look forward to your future. Today may be the day to take the first step and launch yourself afresh into life.

TAKING THE FIRST STEP
An old proverb says, "the journey of a thousand miles begins with a single step". Meditation is a journey of self-discovery. Step out and begin walking as soon as you are ready.

NEW DIRECTION
For many people, starting to meditate is a turning point. It is a new path into the future, which can lead to greater self-knowledge.

9 KEEPING A JOURNAL

Writing a meditation journal is helpful as a record for yourself. Every entry is rather like a snapshot in an album that you can look back on in the future. Keep a note of the meditations you try, and report any problems that you encounter. Summarize each of your experiences, and if possible try to fix the essence of each experience in a single realization.

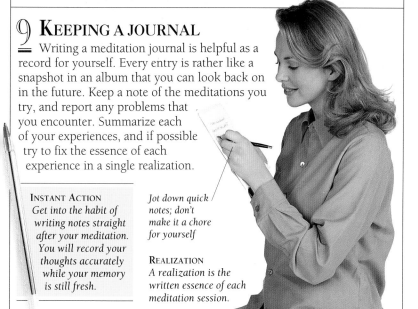

INSTANT ACTION
Get into the habit of writing notes straight after your meditation. You will record your thoughts accurately while your memory is still fresh.

Jot down quick notes; don't make it a chore for yourself

REALIZATION
A realization is the written essence of each meditation session.

13

FIRST STEPS IN MEDITATION

10 CREATING THE RIGHT ENVIRONMENT

The right place in which to meditate depends on your lifestyle and the space you have available. A quiet place which you can return to regularly is ideal. The space should be pleasant, clean, and naturally lit. Keep it simple: an elaborate setting is not necessary. Make your own oasis of calm in which to meditate, and try not to be put off by external factors. There will always be some noise beyond your control. With practice, you will be able to enter a meditative state wherever you are.

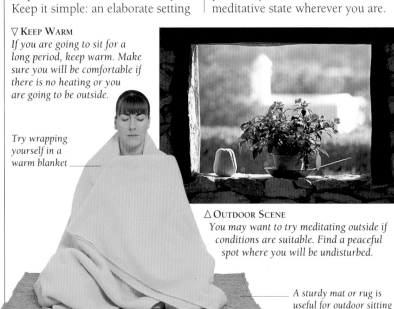

▽ KEEP WARM
If you are going to sit for a long period, keep warm. Make sure you will be comfortable if there is no heating or you are going to be outside.

Try wrapping yourself in a warm blanket

△ OUTDOOR SCENE
You may want to try meditating outside if conditions are suitable. Find a peaceful spot where you will be undisturbed.

A sturdy mat or rug is useful for outdoor sitting

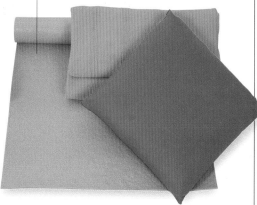

Rug or towel helps if the floor is hard or cold

▽ COMFORTABLE SEAT
Use a cushion for extra comfort if you sit on the floor. Keep a blanket handy to warm yourself up after your meditation.

△ GOOD POSTURE
Try to sit on a hard-backed chair; if you lie down or sit in an armchair, you may fall asleep. Pay attention to your posture (Tip 15).

△ GENTLE RESTORATIVE
You may feel a little light-headed after a long meditation. If so, make sure you have a warm drink.

AVOID DISTRACTIONS
Do whatever you can to minimize obvious distractions; for example, take the phone off the hook. Try not to worry too much about any external noise from neighbours, animals, and children's voices.

11 WHEN NOT TO MEDITATE

Don't attempt to meditate at a time of day that is always busy, or if you are over-stimulated by caffeine or alcohol, since you will probably be distracted. Early morning, when you are fresh, is an excellent time to meditate.

You may fall asleep if you are tired, or after a big meal

12 HOW LONG SHOULD EACH SESSION LAST?

Five minutes daily is a good beginning. A long session will not necessarily provide more benefit than a short one, especially when you have just begun meditating. Short, regular sessions are fine, and certainly better than infrequent long sessions. After some time, you will probably sit for longer periods, and discover the pattern that suits you best.

FIVE MINUTES A DAY

13 BECOMING RELAXED

Relaxation is good preparation for meditation. Sit comfortably (*Tip 15*). Breathe slowly and deeply. Repeat the words below to yourself; feel the tension release.

"The muscles of my head and face are relaxing: I am relaxed ▪ The muscles of my neck are relaxing: I am relaxed ▪ The muscles of my shoulders and chest are relaxing: I am relaxed ▪ The muscles of my arms and hands are relaxing: I am relaxed ▪ The muscles of my legs and feet are relaxing: I am relaxed ▪ I feel relaxed. My mind is calm. My body is calm ▪ I am relaxed. My mind is alert. My mind is awake."

◁ BODY LANGUAGE
A calm mind and body benefit your health and well-being. Your body language will show you are at ease and feeling confident. The routine above will relax your whole body.

SLOW DOWN ▷
Learning to relax is a valuable skill in beating stress. Don't rush the relaxation exercise. With experience, you will not need this preliminary practice.

14 IDENTIFY PHYSICAL TENSION

A great deal of emotional tension is often carried as physical strain in your neck, shoulders, and back. Trying the relaxation exercise (*Tip 13*) may reveal that certain areas of your body remain tense. If you find such areas, try some massage, or help yourself with regular routines like the exercise for head and neck tension shown below, taking care not to strain any muscles. Deep breathing or breath counting (*Tip 17*) can also help relieve tension. Dispelling areas of physical tension will enable you to sit comfortably during meditation.

Push against your hands as hard as possible, and hold

△ REFRESH YOURSELF
Hand-washing is both a practical and symbolic act of preparation. A hot bath is a good tension reliever.

EASE NECK TENSION
This will ease discomfort, especially if you have been sitting for a while. Link hands behind your head, pull shoulders back, and push your head against your hands.

LOOK AT YOUR LIFESTYLE
If you find deep-seated physical tension, look for the reason. Could you add more exercise and relaxation to your routine?

15 SITTING COMFORTABLY

Meditation very often involves sitting quietly. If you are in an uncomfortable position, you will be distracted and find it difficult to sit still. Traditional, cross-legged postures are perfect for long periods of sitting, but they are often achieved after special training and can be hard if you are not supple.

Try to keep your shoulders back and your back upright. You can also kneel on a low bench or a firm cushion. Place your hands carefully (*below*) to stop them fidgeting.

Palms face either up or down on your thighs

CROSS-LEGGED POSITION ▷
Sit on a firm cushion. Place your hands in your lap and lengthen your spine. Close your eyes, or just lower your gaze.

△ **EGYPTIAN POSE**
Try sitting on a hard-backed chair in this pose. It is named after the style of many Egyptian statues.

RELAXED IS BEST
Traditional sitting positions aid meditation by making posture stable, yet relaxed and comfortable.

Comfortable, loose-fitting clothes will help you relax

EASY SITTING
You may find clasping your hands loosely and holding them in your lap the most natural arrangement.

HANDS OF THE BUDDHA
One hand is cupped inside the other. In this position, your thumbs should ideally rest against each other.

INDIAN MUDRA
You could try one of these symbolic hand gestures. For this one, place index fingers against thumbs as shown.

16 BREATHING FROM THE DIAPHRAGM

The act of breathing is barely noticeable. Place one hand on your upper chest for a moment. You will probably feel just a slight rise and fall. To meditate, you will breathe consciously, creating a slow, deep, rhythmic breath cycle using your lungs, abdomen, and diaphragm. Take a long, deep breath through your nose. Your diaphragm descends and your abdomen rises. As you breathe out, the reverse happens. Try to watch each phase in the cycle of a single breath: inhale; pause; exhale; pause.

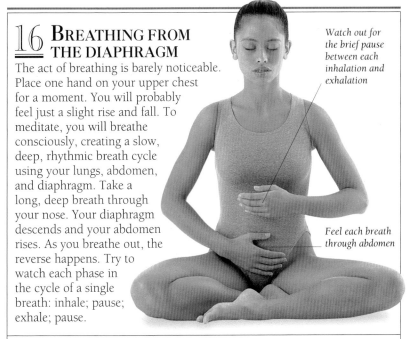

Watch out for the brief pause between each inhalation and exhalation

Feel each breath through abdomen

17 BREATH COUNTING

Breath counting is accepted as a commonly used practice that harmonizes mind and body. The aim is to keep a mental tally of your breaths without losing count or becoming distracted. Count from one to ten and then start again. The simplest method is to inhale and mentally count one, then exhale and count two. Begin again when you reach ten. You could also try counting a complete inhalation and exhalation cycle as one.

If you lose count of your breaths, simply start again

Breath counting may sound easy, but you will find it quite challenging

GOOD TRAINING
Meditation trains your mind to be more observant. Your breath is a perfect subject.

18 GOING IN TO MEDITATION

This brings physiological and mental changes. It means moving from one state of mind and body to another as if you are crossing a symbolic threshold. Choose a pose to sit in. When you feel calm and relaxed, sitting comfortably, with your breathing deep and rhythmic, imagine yourself passing over the threshold. Beyond it, bring the subject of your meditation to mind. See if you find the image helpful.

OPEN DOOR
Visualize the doorway as you prepare with relaxation and correct posture and breathing.

With practice, you can enter instantly, but when meditation is new, your entry will be slower

19 WHAT IF YOU ARE DISTRACTED?

As you meditate, you will soon discover numerous mental distractions. Your thoughts seem to wander without warning. Try not to follow the false trail. Gently bring your mind back to your chosen subject. You will need to do this repeatedly. Although it can be very disheartening, it happens to everyone. Be patient with yourself.

20 COMING OUT OF MEDITATION

Return to the state of mind and body that fits everyday life. When you have finished with your subject, release your concentration, dissolve any images from your mind, and note anything you want to remember. Mentally cross the threshold and take a few moments to readjust. Allow your body to return to its normal breathing rhythm. Take a while to refocus yourself on the external world.

Take your time when coming out of meditation, especially at first. It will be quicker with practice

CLOSED DOOR
At the end of your session, see yourself crossing the threshold back out into the external world.

21 How to go deeper

Imagine yourself exploring an ancient castle with many rooms and doors. Eventually, you come to a door with your name marked on it. Opening it, you find a spiral staircase. Descend the staircase.

Take your time. Use all your senses to imagine the scene clearly. The staircase will take you deeply into yourself, since the castle represents the whole person. Reverse the journey to end your meditation.

CONTINUE THE JOURNEY
When you are at the bottom of the staircase, imagine a peaceful room where you can rest. Furnish it as you wish.

YOUR INNER WORLD
You have already visualized the inner doorway. Use the same ability to go further in meditation.

22 Going forward

The results of each session of meditation can be compared to droplets of water falling into a container. Each droplet is tiny on its own, but in time they add up to create a noticeable change. Every meditation session produces a tiny alteration. These changes are often quite invisible on their own. You may even wonder if anything at all is happening as a result of your practice. Don't be discouraged by this; any changes will gradually become apparent. In reality, you are making progress all the time.

RIPPLE EFFECT
Every "droplet" of meditation practice creates ripples that will affect your life.

SYMBOLS & IMAGERY

23 WHAT IS A SYMBOL?

A symbol conveys meaning without words. Each one may have a variety of interpretations. Modern symbols, such as computer icons, are often instructional. Older symbols convey ideas. Some, like the Jewish menorah, are specific to one tradition. Others, like rings, which express eternal love, are universal. They are like a shared language. See them as short cuts to a particular subject for meditation.

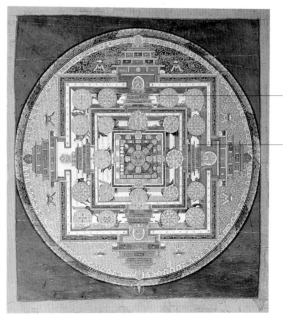

TIBETAN MANDALA
Each colour, section, and figure in this symbolic map of the universe has meaning.

A mandala usually describes states of mind and being

A meditator travels through the world of the mandala as if it were a real place

IDEAS IN PICTURES
Meditation uses many symbols to help you think deeply about abstract ideas and concepts such as love, time, wisdom, or interdependence.

24 TRADITIONAL SYMBOLS

EVERGREEN LEAVES

Every culture has its own traditional symbols that convey spiritual, religious, or social ideas. A lighted candle is a universal symbol of peace and hope. In the West, evergreens, such as bay and spruce, represent continuing life. Food is often symbolic too. In the East, rice means life and abundance. Think about the traditional symbols that have meaning for you.

ROSE WINDOW ▷
A rose window brings light into many Christian cathedrals, combining the symbolic circle and rose. It is like a mandala of the West.

SYMBOL OF PEACE & HOPE

25 SYMBOLS IN NATURE

The countless symbols that come from nature are part of the universal language of world mythology, folklore, and legend. Nature offers geographical features, sea and sky, and recurring patterns. Worldwide, the sun represents the source of life; the moon, growth and cycles of time. A mountain means strength and endurance. Aspects of nature may have other attributes for you.

NATURAL POWER
The waterfall symbolizes a place of power and creation; a river represents the flow of life. Water also means fertility and purity.

26 DISCOVER YOUR OWN SYMBOLS

The shared symbolic history of humanity is fascinating: it's like a common secret language. Seek out a variety of images (which may be common to different cultures) in art, architecture, artefacts – and even in fairy tales. Choose a symbol and try to follow it through different traditions in myth and folklore. You will discover the past significance of your chosen symbol and what it means to you now. Many symbols like the dragon, eye, snake, or moon, are very ancient.

27 OPENING YOUR MIND'S EYE

How often do you really use your mind's eye? You can describe memories or experiences in words, but with visualization, you can also create descriptive pictures in your imagination. Test the difference. Say the word "rose", and you might find just a few associations. Then call to mind the image of a rose in bud. Attempt to recreate it as fully as you can. Now, in your mind's eye, allow the bud to open into a flower. See the colour of the petals and imagine their softness. As you hold the image of the rose, what other associations come to mind? The more you use your creative imagination, the more vivid it will become. Exercising your mind's eye will help you use imagery in meditation. Close this exercise by simply allowing the image to fade.

Smell the perfume of the rose in your imagination

THINK VISUALLY
Visualizing is just a way of thinking. The more you use your mind's eye, the more helpful it will be in meditation and your ordinary life.

28 REDISCOVERING YOUR IMAGINATION

Some meditations ask you to create pictures in your mind's eye. This exercise will introduce you to using your imagination visually and without constraint. See yourself holding a white disc in your hand. Write your name on it and throw it into the sky. Watch it rising up until you are dazzled by the brightness of the sky. The disc disappears from view. When you next look, you see a white bird soaring above you. Watch the bird in the sky. Something is falling out of the sky towards you. Your hand reaches out to catch a crystal egg. The bird is nowhere to be seen. When you look more closely at the crystal, you see that an image of a white bird is carved inside.

FLIGHT OF FANCY
Children have vivid imaginations; keep yours alive. Try creating an inner landscape (Tip 32).

INNER IMAGES
If a meditation does not use a symbol or image, concentration and awareness will help you to follow relevant thoughts.

29 FOLLOWING A THOUGHT

Meditation is inwardly active. Your mind must keep focused on its subject. This means following wanted thoughts while letting unwanted ones pass. Following a thought requires concentration. Holding a symbol in your mind's eye can act like an anchor each time your mind is distracted. You can come back to this definite image. Watch the image and begin to collect the associations you have with your subject. The constant image helps you to keep returning to your chosen subject.

CONSTANT SYMBOL
ANCHORS SUBJECT

30 THINKING WITH PICTURES

Thinking with pictures can be a useful skill. It makes visual meditations easier to create and can help with all sorts of tasks. Think in pictures to remember items on a list, to furnish a room, lay out a garden, or prepare a schedule; you will find plenty of other uses. Your ability will improve the more often you exercise it. So, when the phone rings, see the caller in your mind. Next time you read a novel or listen to an audio-tape, stretch your imagination and think in pictures.

31 WHAT IF YOU FIND IT HARD TO VISUALIZE?

If visualizing does not come naturally or easily to you, you can also call an image to mind by drawing on your senses of hearing, touch, and even smell and taste. Your memory is full of experiences and sensations that you can use. Can you bring to mind the scent of sea air, or the sound a boot makes crunching on snow? Experiment to find which of the five senses you feel most comfortable with.

VIVID INSIGHT
The more senses you employ, the more vivid your inner experiences will be.

Touch: with your eyes closed, can you recall the feel of an animal's soft fur?

Sound: can you hear the sound of an instrument playing in your imagination?

Taste: can you distinguish different tastes in your mind?

Smell: can you recall a flower's scent from memory?

32 TAKING AN INNER JOURNEY

Read the journey here and then create the inner landscape in your mind. You are standing at a gate that leads into a field. Walking ahead, you see a single tree. What does it look like? Touch the bark and then pick a leaf. Finally, sit with your back against the trunk and meditate upon the tree itself. To close, retrace your steps and let the image dissolve.

See the detail as well as the larger picture

33 RELEASE YOUR CREATIVITY

Meditation sharpens all your senses. This will help you become more observant and aware in daily life. You can discover and nurture your own creativity by developing your imagination (*Tips 23–32*) and using your visualization skill.

Creativity takes many forms; finding your own way of creative expression is part of the process of self-development. Discovering your creative self can be very rewarding, and will help you to deal positively with the different demands of life.

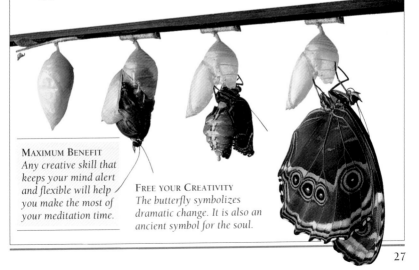

MAXIMUM BENEFIT
Any creative skill that keeps your mind alert and flexible will help you make the most of your meditation time.

FREE YOUR CREATIVITY
The butterfly symbolizes dramatic change. It is also an ancient symbol for the soul.

27

NOT THINKING AT ALL

34 ZAZEN

Zazen means "just sitting". This is a central practice of Zen Buddhism. It is most often done facing a wall to avoid distractions. No images or symbols, thoughts, ideas, or words are used as subjects for this type of meditation. The aim of zazen is just to observe what is happening in your mind, without becoming sidetracked by your own thoughts. Instead, concentrate on breath counting (*Tip 17*). Watch your breath with full awareness. Try not to think at all. Tips 35–41 will help you to discipline your thoughts and find peace of mind.

ZEN GARDEN
This monk contemplates a Zen garden. The carefully raked gravel lines are themselves subjects for meditation.

THE MONKEY
IS NEVER STILL

35 THE CHATTERING MONKEY

Buddhism compares an untrained mind to a chattering monkey that jumps from one branch to another. The monkey is never still but constantly moving. This is not a flattering image, but if you watch your thoughts darting from one random idea to another, you may discover that it is quite accurate. You can train yourself to be aware of the stream of thoughts passing through your head, and quiet the chattering monkey.

36 YOUR STREAM OF CONSCIOUSNESS

Think of all that flows through your mind as the stream of your consciousness. Sit quietly, turn your attention inward, and just watch your thoughts as they arrive and depart. Try this for a few minutes. At first, you may be very self-conscious, but soon your thoughts will become more natural. You might be surprised at what you discover in a short time: distant memories, future plans, or quite unexpected images.

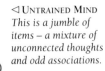

◁ UNTRAINED MIND
This is a jumble of items – a mixture of unconnected thoughts and odd associations.

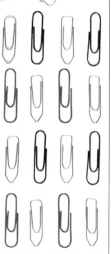

TRAINED MIND ▷
Watching the flow of your thoughts, and developing some detachment, is a first step in creating order within your mind.

◁ TAKE NOTE
At the end of the session, jot down what you can remember.

37 IS JUST SITTING A WASTE OF TIME?

Sitting still may feel very strange at first, particularly if you are usually busy. However, it is a mistake to think that sitting still is the same as doing nothing. You are retraining your mind to be more effective and creative in the long run. Short periods of inner quiet will refresh your mind and body. Far from wasting time, you are making good use of a short time. Time spent on this is beneficial. Don't let guilt get the better of you. Take time out – just for yourself.

29

38 NOT FOLLOWING A THOUGHT

Have you ever looked into your mind? Try watching your stream of consciousness flowing at full speed. This flow never stops, but you can practise developing detachment from your thoughts.

See them as clouds passing across the sky, or even as items on a conveyor belt. Each thought will bring new associations in its wake. Be aware of this, but let your thoughts pass and try not to follow.

IF PASSING THOUGHTS CATCH YOUR ATTENTION, LET THEM DRIFT AWAY & DEPART

39 FINDING SPACE

Do you feel that your head is crowded with unwanted thoughts? If so, you need to find mental space. When you observe your thoughts, be aware of the short space between the end of one thought and the start of another. Look for this momentary pause, no matter how brief. Mentally attempt to rest in this space. With practice, you will be able to expand it, and your sense of an overcrowded mind will lessen.

TAKE YOUR TIME
Don't try finding space until you have observed your thoughts (Tip 38). Practise slowly and create a firm foundation on which to build gradually.

MAKING SPACE IN YOUR MIND BRINGS MENTAL CLARITY & OPENNESS

40 THE SILENT MOMENT

It may seem impossible to escape from noise in today's busy world. Everyday sounds must be accepted, but give silence a place in your life. Remember that it can be restful, and make an effort to establish silence once in a while. When the chance arises at home, deliberately choose silence for a short time. You may use the radio or television as company or distraction: try silence instead. This practice will help you when you cannot escape noise. Meditation retreats invariably include periods of restful silence.

LEAVE NOISE BEHIND
Experiencing silence will encourage you to listen with greater attention to the many sounds that surround you.

41 PEACE AT LAST

This gentle exercise aims to harmonize mind and body. Sit comfortably, keeping warm if you are outside. Relax deeply and fully. Enter your own meditative state, using breath counting (*Tip 17*) to focus on your breath. When thoughts arise, just watch them pass through your mind. Sit with a quiet mind and continue to watch your breath. Peace is possible, even in a busy and demanding world.

TRANQUIL PLACE
Take advantage of any beautiful natural space to practise meditating quietly outdoors.

MAXIMUM BENEFIT
The more often you can sit quietly, the more you will be able to take the quality of peacefulness into life.

MEDITATING WITH COLOURS

42 WHY COLOURS?

Colour carries meaning for all of us, although meanings vary among cultures. Its symbolism is universal, often practical, as in red for danger. Emotional qualities have also come to be associated with certain colours: red means anger and passion. To draw upon the qualities of a particular colour, visualize it clearly in your mind's eye. Imagine it as fully as you can in all its depth and richness while also reflecting upon and trying to assume the qualities you seek.

△ RARE SIGHT
Rainbows are considered lucky, perhaps because they contain all the colours in the spectrum and therefore all their qualities.

COLOUR WHEEL
Think about the qualities you would like to enhance in yourself. Choose a colour to focus on.

UNIVERSAL REFERENCE
You are always surrounded by colours. Tips 43–53 can help you to harness their powerful associations in meditation.

43 RED: STRENGTH

Red – the colour of blood – is associated with the power of life itself. In the distant past, red ochre pigment was used at traditional burial ceremonies to signify new life beyond physical death. Red is often thought of as a hot colour. It brings the qualities of physical strength, power, passion, and energetic drive to mind. Red can be overpowering when used for home interiors, but it is a very popular colour for cars, which represent energy and power.

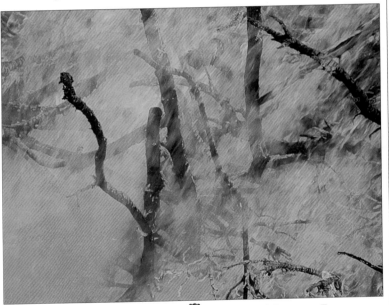

RED ATTRIBUTES
Draw upon the strong,
forceful qualities of red
in your meditation.
This will help at times
when you lack drive,
direction, energy,
or courage.

△ POWERFUL FORCE
Red almost always makes
you think of fire; both mean
danger. Warning signs are
often marked in red.

Red in nature is a
strong colour: it
attracts or warns

44 ORANGE: VITALITY

Orange is a warm colour, although not so strong as red. Orange is an enlivening colour. It stimulates enjoyment and vitality, fun and movement. Orange is associated with the warm glow of sunset, and with tropical fruit and exotic flowers. It is often connected with sunny climates and sun-loving people. Orange offers you brilliance and vibrancy, activity and involvement. Draw on this colour and its qualities if you want to break down barriers, discover enthusiasm within yourself, and get more fun out of life.

BRILLIANT GLOW
Watching the sun set in the evening can be wonderful if the sky is filled briefly with orange tones and hues.

HILLSIDE REVIVAL
Yellow seems to be everywhere in spring as the earth awakens after winter.

45 YELLOW: CLARITY

Yellow lacks the warmth of the emotional colours, although it is the colour of the sun. It is the most visible of all the colours, and is used internationally for signs. Yellow is linked with mental activity and the creative inspiration that comes from a clear and open mind. It is associated with mental development and the use of abstract ideas. When your mind is confused, let in a ray of sunlight. Draw upon yellow and its qualities if you seek clarity in your thinking, for example when you face a big decision.

46 GREEN: RENEWAL

Green is the predominant colour of the natural world. You may see it so often that you forget to notice its many shades. Natural green is the pigment chlorophyll, which helps plants absorb light energy to manufacture food. It is therefore essential for plant life – an example of a natural link between a colour and light. Green is also the colour of spring, when more daylight encourages new growth after winter. In meditation, draw on green as the colour of new growth, renewal, and healing.

◁ SPOILT FOR CHOICE
Green is the colour of nature's own growth. Open your eyes to the many different greens in the natural world.

THE COLOUR
OF RENEWAL

GREEN ATTRIBUTES
Draw upon green and its qualities for a fresh start, to open up new opportunities, or to undertake personal growth in some aspect of your life.

GREEN MOVEMENT ▷
Environmentalists have adopted the colour green as the symbol of conservation and respect for all life.

Green is often the colour of camouflage

47 BLUE: RELAXATION

Blue is associated with a state of relaxed well-being and peacefulness. It also has celestial significance: ancient Egyptians valued the deep blue mineral, lapis lazuli, sometimes flecked with gold, which they saw as an image of the heavens; some Russian Orthodox churches have blue, gold-starred domes. In meditation, these connections may help you feel calm, peaceful, and reflective too.

Draw upon blue and its qualities when you feel tense, stressed, or under pressure

BLUE UNIVERSE
Seen in creatures of the air such as butterflies and birds, the colour blue appears especially dazzling and ethereal.

△ **THE BIG BLUE**
We see blue in the oceans of the world. This is an illusion, since water reflects the colour of the sky. The world appears very blue, seen from space.

48 INDIGO: DEDICATION

This deep purple-blue is a rich, dark colour. It is rare in nature and hard to extract, and therefore signifies hidden depths, mystery, and secrecy. In the past, spiritual traditions such as meditation have often been secret. Indigo's rarity has given rise to associations with imperial power and religion. Indigo signifies a commitment to spiritual values, human potential, and the expansion of the mind.

INDIGO ATTRIBUTES
Draw upon indigo and its qualities in meditation if you feel the need to renew your dedication to a spiritual path or to seek new avenues of personal service.

49 VIOLET: HARMONY

Violet is a colour of clarity and lightness. It is the final colour of the rainbow and the opposite of red, which is apparent by its qualities. The colour violet suggests the sensitivity of the spirit, and stands for the universal, rather than the individual and the personal. Violet soothes your passions by expressing a shared unity and harmony.

Enjoy the colour violet through the short-lived iris

VIOLET ATTRIBUTES
Draw upon violet and its qualities when you feel able to shed your personal needs and wants in favour of universal peace for humanity.

Nature is sparing in its use of indigo

37

50 WHITE: WHOLENESS

White light is composed of all seven colours of the rainbow, so it symbolizes wholeness and spiritual purity. A white flag means truce, therefore peace. White has varying associations, but it is universally related to rites of passage. Newborn babies, brides, and the deceased may be clothed in white. It is worn for religious rites of entry into spiritual life, such as baptism and confirmation. These moments of passing into new life express a belief in universal spiritual truths.

PURE WHITE
Call white images to mind to reinforce your sense of wholeness and purity.

51 SILVER: INTUITION

Silver is compared to the light of the moon. It represents the subconscious mind, including your dream life and hidden feelings. The moon's light is gentle, and so such areas inevitably remain somewhat concealed. The silver moon figures largely in mythology, where it represents the mysterious, hidden forces of the mind and spirit.

◁ SILVER LIGHT
The moon often signifies the feminine, which may be naturally intuitive. With silver, explore your subconscious life.

Silvery pearl is linked to the feminine and the moon

52 GOLD: ASPIRATION

Gold never deteriorates. It is a universal symbol of perfection and eternity. It signifies the undying part of human nature, the soul itself. Every civilization has reserved gold for its most important artefacts. Sacred statues and religious objects have been made from gold to express divinity for the community. Draw upon gold and its qualities to express your spiritual nature.

GOLD ATTRIBUTES
When you wish to offer the highest and the best of yourself to a shared cause, meditate on gold. Let your aspiration shine.

TARNISHED IMAGE
Gold can inspire greed when its monetary value becomes supreme.

Most precious of metals and sign of greatest value

53 RAINBOW LIGHT EXERCISE

You can meditate on the rainbow as a symbol of potential. Imagine sitting beneath its arc. See the bands of colour brilliantly. As you build each colour, reflect upon the qualities it represents. Finally, meditate on all of the colours as indicators of your future potential. You can meditate on the individual colours by visualizing each as a sphere of light at specific locations in your body (*below*).

Violet light shows your spiritual sense and consciousness

Blue light, near your throat, affects communication

Yellow light rests where you nourish yourself. It shows your dynamic will

Red light reveals your awareness of, and confidence in, your physical body

Indigo light rests with intuition and dream life; here, both sides of the brain work together

Green light, found in the heart area, represents the awakening and health of love

Orange sheds light on reproduction, sexuality, and your openness to others

AWARENESS IN EVERY MOMENT

54 MINDFUL LIVING

Every day is composed of ordinary moments. You can choose to remember or to forget these little incidents. Forgetting is easy – it is much harder to remember. Try to recall what you were doing mid-morning yesterday. What have you done today? Notice each moment as it happens, and bring life fully into your awareness. Using this section of the book, start capturing every moment of every day.

△ NOTHING TOO SMALL
Living mindfully is about paying close attention to everything you are involved in. Nothing is too insignificant to observe.

BENEFICIAL STATE OF MIND
You'll learn quickly, recall effectively, and get the most out of every situation.

Doing the most ordinary task mindfully lets you notice each moment as it unfolds

55 THE OBSERVING SELF

How well do you know yourself? Mindful living includes developing self-observation. Try to watch everything you do as though through an observer's eyes. This is rather like having an inner witness. Observing yourself aims to bring objectivity to your life. Seeing your reactions and responses will teach you a great deal about yourself.

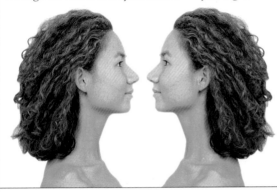

WITNESS YOURSELF
Self-awareness grows from observing yourself mindfully. You become the subject of your own meditation. Try not to judge yourself. Simply watch and observe.

56 WATCHING YOUR BREATH

Try mindful breathing. Sit comfortably in meditation and focus your attention on detecting the physical touch of your breath. This may be just above your upper lip or at the tip of your nose. Just breathe normally, but keep your mind concentrated on the sensation of the touch of the air. As you breathe in, repeat "In", and as you breathe out, repeat "Out" to yourself, to keep your mind focused. Try this for five minutes.

CALMLY AWARE
Mindful breathing will help you develop both calmness and awareness. Concentrate on breathing evenly and deeply.

Focus on detecting the feel of your breath

Mindfulness of breathing is important in Buddhist practice

57 WATCHING YOUR BODY

Think of this process as getting to know your physical self: don't mistake this for your whole self. Become aware of how you move at any given moment. How do you carry yourself in each different situation? Your body mirrors your state of mind. Observe your body language with objectivity and learn to understand it. What does your body express now – joy or burden, worry or peace, fear or freedom?

STEP BY STEP
Watch your body move to accomplish a simple physical act. You could begin by observing the sequence of a single step.

CAREFUL NOTATION
Be aware of everything that happens. In any situation, ask yourself what you are directly experiencing and feeling.

58 WATCHING YOUR RESPONSES

This means simply noting your responses to experiences as they arise. Do you like or dislike certain things, or are you indifferent? Become aware of all these reactions and responses. You will gain self-awareness when you are conscious of everything you do, think, and feel. You may respond in ways that are expected or required. If you do this all the time, you suppress the direct experience, and your own responses. At first, observing your responses may seem artificial, but with regular use it becomes natural and easy. Try it for a short period.

59 WATCHING HOW YOU FEEL

Aim to increase your self-knowledge by observing your emotions. Watch your different states of mind as they arise. Actions often take place without thought; patterns of behaviour are repeated, leaving no opportunity for change. Self-awareness gives you a different view. You can see the patterns and change them yourself, choosing how to behave or react at any given point. So stop and look at yourself.

WHOSE FAULT?
Try not to see a confrontation in terms of blame or fault. You will understand your reactions more easily as they happen.

LOOK HONESTLY
You might find guilt, fear, or envy when you examine your emotions, but take time to recognize your good qualities too.

60 INSIGHT – THE GIFT OF MEDITATION

Insight is like a direct view into yourself. It feels like a sudden moment of great clarity. It brings a valuable new perspective on life, and a deep sense of knowing that is not based on formal learning. You can gain insight by practising mindfulness in life. As you observe yourself, you will see more clearly. A moment of insight is a personal experience. This can bring you a new way of looking at the world.

OUTER & INNER WELL-BEING

61 HEALTH & VITALITY

Your physical health is closely related to your emotional and psychological state. The new awareness that comes from meditation will help you to look more deeply at all aspects of your life. Think about your well-being by asking yourself:

- do you sleep well?
- do you have good reserves of stamina and energy?
- do you have any recurring minor illnesses such as coughs and colds?
- do you take regular exercise?
- do you eat a balanced diet?
- do you have any addictive habits, for example smoking?

◁ ENERGY BOOST
Fitness will give you a positive outlook, greater energy, and help prevent minor ailments.

VICIOUS CIRCLE ▷
Do you wake feeling tired? If you are run down, you may be unable to unwind to get the rest you need.

Try to take a little exercise, perhaps a brisk walk, every day

TIME TO CHANGE?
The questions above will help you reflect on your overall health and consider changes you might make.

62 ASSESS YOUR EMOTIONAL WELL-BEING

Your ability to communicate and sustain healthy relationships is an essential part of your emotional well-being. Pause to consider your emotional health. Ask yourself:
- do you make and keep long-term friendships and relationships?
- are you a good friend, parent, partner, son, or daughter?
- can you express feelings of love and tenderness to others?
- can you deal with anger?
- can you accept forgiveness, and forgive yourself and others?

SHARE THE BURDEN
Talking to friends is a good way to cope with difficult feelings. Are you a good listener?

ASK FOR HELP
Don't be afraid to seek support for emotional problems. Therapy, self-help groups, and counselling can help.

63 BLOCKED EMOTIONS

Meditation can help you become more aware of the links between your body, thoughts, and feelings. When you do not express your feelings at the right time, they may be stored inwardly instead, becoming an invisible burden. This creates frustration and resentment. Eventually, you may not be able to contain your feelings. Try to let go of small annoyances, and express others calmly.

INCOMMUNICADO
Not communicating does not solve a problem. Sometimes, a third party can help. Meditation will enable you to know yourself better.

64 THE ARMOURED BODY

Your mind and body are a unity. When they are in harmony, you feel well. Everything from your life's journey is recorded in your body. Emotional pain can manifest itself as a blockage, in which life energy does not flow freely. See "life energy" as the river of your life. It should flow through your body dynamically, but sometimes becomes choked and sluggish. This may happen so gradually you will not notice. Treatments to restore your natural energy balance, like acupuncture or shiatsu massage, can be wonderfully invigorating.

Your throat *houses your voice. Problems here can arise from not saying what you mean. Swallowing your words stifles your own creative expression*

Breathing *difficulties can reflect deep shock. You may carry on as normal, but a trauma literally "takes your breath away"*

Your legs *support you. Lower leg ailments may reveal fear of moving into the future. In the upper legs, ailments can mean childhood traumas*

With your feet, *you step out into life. Foot problems symbolize anxieties about the future – do you go with caution or confidence?*

Your head *is rather like your control centre. Self-criticism and harsh judgements produce tension and headaches*

Do you shoulder *many responsibilities? Stress often shows in bad posture and muscular tension in shoulders, neck, and back*

Your stomach *may be sensitive to your emotional state. "Butterflies" in the stomach signify anxiety. You must digest life experiences; when you've had enough, you might say, "I can't stomach it"*

WATCH YOURSELF
Bodily illness may reflect life events, but remember to consult your medical practitioner about any physical symptoms.

65 CONTROLLING STRESS

Positive stress is healthy – it motivates and helps you achieve success. However, stress from competing external factors may be a burden. Can you cope with any conflicting demands in your life? Reduce harmful stress by redefining your aims and daily objectives. When you are ready, slow down: find a new outlook, value yourself, and start to live differently. Ten minutes of relaxation a day can make a big difference to the way you feel.

SIGNS OF HARMFUL STRESS
When your stress levels rise, your pulse rate goes up, blood pressure increases, breathing becomes faster, and you may start to perspire.

66 STRETCH & RELEASE

As tension is reflected in your body, you can benefit from soothing taut areas before it becomes locked in. Stretching exercises can help remove habitual tension caused by holding the same position all day at work. A massage is a particularly relaxing way of dispelling more deeply felt tension. You might also try classes in the Alexander Technique, which will teach you to move consciously and avoid further damage.

HEALING HANDS
Rolfing is a method of deep, intensive massage, designed to release especially deep emotional blocks from the past. Make sure you use a fully qualified practitioner.

67 MOVING MEDITATIONS

Meditation can take many forms. It may be active, when mind and body are united by conscious awareness. Different cultures have applied this principle. Both yoga (from India) and t'ai chi ch'uan (from China) integrate your mind and body through visualization, breathing, and movement. Such ancient practices engage your universal life force (Indian *prana* or Chinese *chi*). Consequently, these dynamic body–mind systems are beneficial to the whole person.

◁ T'AI CHI CH'UAN
Relaxed, balanced movements are used to co-ordinate mind and body. Practice benefits both self-awareness and general health.

Wear loose, comfortable clothes to practise

Attend to all the elements of each pose

△ YOGA
Yoga harmonizes your mind, body, breath, and spirit. Every pose takes concentration.

Life expresses itself through movement

NATURAL BALANCE
Body–mind systems have many benefits. They give flexibility and suppleness, and develop your mental alertness. Practice actively balances your life force. Why not join a class?

DANCING ▷
Dance has also been used as a vehicle for meditation. See it as an opportunity to express yourself.

Enjoy moving through dance and just do it for yourself

68 THE FOUNTAIN OF LIFE

Imagine a pool deep in the earth that is a source of vitality and energy. Breathe in, and feel this energy as liquid light passing into your body through the soles of your feet, up your legs, and into your spine. When this liquid light reaches the top of your head, it rises like a fountain. As you breathe out, feel this energy cascading back to the ground to be reabsorbed into the pool. On each in-breath, feel invigorated; on each out-breath, feel cleansed.

INVIGORATING EXERCISE
This meditation should be done for a cycle of three complete breaths. Try this when you want to feel actively energized and cleansed – perhaps as preparation for a moving meditation.

INVIGORATING & CLEANSING

REFRESHING FOUNTAIN
Renew your energy by creating your inner courtyard. Make it a place you can revisit.

69 REVITALIZING EXERCISE

This exercise will give you a quick energy boost during the day. Sit comfortably. See yourself dressed quite differently, in clothes that suit your inner self. When you are ready, imagine yourself standing in a beautiful courtyard filled with exotic flowers and vines. The air is warm. In the centre is a fountain, pouring crystal clear water, and hung with assorted drinking cups. Step forward, choose a cup, and fill it from the fountain. Let this drink fill your mind, body, and spirit with new life and vitality.

MEDITATING ON THE WORLD

70 ANCIENT COSMOLOGY

To be curious about the greater world of the stars and planets is natural. Every culture explains the origin and nature of the universe in its own ideas. The four elements, and the quality of spirit, have been used for this purpose in East and West. Tibetan Buddhism describes universal forces using the mandala (*Tip 23*), a symbolic pattern of relationships. These patterns may be painted, built, or made of coloured sand. Sacred buildings and burial places, such as Buddhist stupas, often contain cosmic symbols.

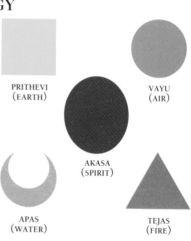

PRITHEVI
(EARTH)

VAYU
(AIR)

AKASA
(SPIRIT)

APAS
(WATER)

TEJAS
(FIRE)

△ EASTERN TATTVAS
These elemental symbols (tattvas) are used for meditation. They are also combined to make more complicated symbols.

◁ SACRED ARCHITECTURE
In the Great Stupa at Sanchi, India, the dome represents the heavens enclosing the earth. The temple contains stone-carved cosmic symbols.

Earth: *the five-pointed star stands for an outstretched human form set in the circle of the earth. It represents earth and the quality of sensation*

Fire: *the rod represents fire. Its spark suggests the fire of the higher mind, intuition*

Air: *the sword cuts and divides. It represents air and the mind, separating thoughts with clarity*

WESTERN SYMBOLS ▷
The ancient Greeks first described the four elements. Later, alchemists related the elements to the four natural humours. The Holy Grail stands for the search for spirit in life.

Water: *a cup or goblet stands for the element of water and the quality of emotion*

◁ ALL FOUR ELEMENTS
When you meditate on the elements, you will find that you cannot really separate them. This is an example of the interdependence of all things in the universe.

INFINITE SPACE
The sky is a place of great activity. Look at the stars. Meditate on the vastness of universal life.

71 EARTH, AIR, WATER, & FIRE

The components of earth, air, water, and fire frequently appear in cosmic models, ancient and modern. These elements, with the addition of spirit, light, and space, are still a customary starting place in many types of meditation: look closely and you will see them everywhere. Each one is associated with particular qualities. When you draw upon these in meditation, you might like to place an example of the real element nearby, or call to mind a symbol that represents that quality (*Tip 70*). Meditating on the elements will develop your awareness of the everyday world.

AS ABOVE, SO BELOW
The ancients coined this phrase to define the unity of the universe. In addition to the 109 elements, modern physicists have now discovered the unifying subatomic world.

OLD AS THE HILLS
Nature's timescale puts everything into perspective. How old is a mountain?

72 EARTH: PUTTING DOWN ROOTS

Some traditions see the physical world merely as a stepping stone on the journey to a future life in another world. Despite this, being aware of your relationship with the earth will place your consciousness in the here and now. You will get the most out of everyday life and put down your roots firmly into the body of the earth. Do you feel cut off from or connected to life? In meditation, call to mind images of the earth: mountains and deserts, valleys and plains, fertile fields and barren rock. You could fill a bowl with earth to start this meditation.

73 AIR: LETTING GO OF OLD IDEAS

Air is invisible, yet essential. The air is never still, but ideas can become too fixed. Is it time to let the wind of change blow through your mind? As you meditate on air, try to visualize various images, of a gentle breeze or gale, a whirlwind or a dust storm. Change can be turbulent when it is unexpected. Meditation is a tool that helps you to review your ideas constantly. Let them go before any storm breaks.

AIR POWER
Try lighting a stick of incense for this meditation. Watch the smoke gently rising into the air.

74 WATER: RELEASING TRUE FEELINGS

You are composed largely of water. It has many important properties: water cleanses, sustains, quenches thirst, and refreshes the body. It is essential for all life. Water naturally relates to feelings; you may find you cry with extremes of emotion. Just like water, emotions can be deep, crystal clear, or blocked. Which describes your feelings? In this meditation, call to mind images of rivers and waterfalls, streams and oceans, lakes and raindrops.

ESSENTIAL ELEMENT
Try opening your meditation by setting a bowl of clear water in front of you.

75 FIRE: DYNAMIC CHANGE

Fire occurs naturally, and always brings dynamic change with it. Fire has many different qualities. It gives light and heat; it purifies and consumes; it is dangerous, yet necessary. In meditation, bring to mind images of the volcano and the forest fire, the hearth fire and the bonfire, the funeral pyre, the beacon fire, and the single flame. Sometimes, you may need to burn out the old before the new can appear.

Fire is a warning that can herald both destruction and healing

FOCAL POINT
Lighting a candle is a universal spiritual act. Consider looking at a flame as you meditate on fire.

△ FORCE FOR CHANGE
Fire is often constructive in the long run, despite the widespread damage it may cause. Volcanic action can create new areas of land.

76 SPIRIT: INTERDEPENDENCE

The four primary elements can be seen as aspects of a fifth quality, spirit. You cannot discover spirit through your five senses. It is universal, but you will never see it directly. You cannot understand it, yet all life depends upon it. Spirit shows how all the elements are linked. Love, too, is invisible, but still a part of your everyday life. You find meaning and connection in giving and receiving love. Meditate on universal love as a way to think about spirit's qualities.

77 LIGHT: INNER CLARITY

You may rarely think about natural light, but long periods of darkness or bad light can adversely affect your mood and perspective. Reflect upon the need for light. Think about the transition between night and day, and the different light of each season. Visualize images of a prism, a rainbow, a brilliant sky, or sunshine. Try to become more aware of the quality of light in your life each day.

CLEAR REFLECTION
Your mind is like a mirror. You can mentally "clean" this mirror to reflect reality more clearly.

UNIVERSAL ASSET
Natural light alters in quality as the day lengthens. This response shows the integrity of the natural world.

78 SPACE: FINDING INFINITE POSSIBILITIES

Space is another abstract quality that you might not notice until your own space is restricted. Wide open spaces have a special quality, and this can give you a new perspective on the thoughts that crowd your mind daily. In your meditation, see the infinity of the sky, the scope of an empty landscape, and the unlimited possibilities of the mind itself.

FIND SPACE INSIDE
Your mind is as infinite as space. Its only boundaries are those you have created yourself.

LIVING THROUGH MEDITATION

79 STEPPING OUT

Meditation is about more than sitting at home in a reflective frame of mind. It means making connections to everyday life. Take your meditative mind with you wherever you go. Be observant, be perceptive, and be aware of all that is happening around you as it takes place. Take the positive benefits of meditation with you every day.

HUSTLE & BUSTLE
Meditation is never about escaping from life. So join in with gusto, but carry your awareness with you.

NEW VIEW
Take mindfulness into everyday life and you will see so much more in every situation.

80 OPEN EYES, OPEN HEART

Meditation will wake up your heart and mind. You should see more clearly, understand more effectively, and feel fully. The more you notice, the more you will see. Your deeper perception offers you a greater connection with life. Try not to "sleepwalk" through the day. Open your eyes to everything, and be fully engaged in all of your activities. When you see with open eyes, your heart will open too.

81 FINDING BEAUTY IN LIFE

It is sometimes difficult to find beauty in the world, but wherever you live, with your new perception you can see beauty in the small, the everyday, and the insignificant. Become aware of nature's different colours, textures, and sounds. Look at everything with fresh eyes, and just see things as they are. Cherish a thoughtful gesture. Feel pride in completing a tedious task. You will be able to find something good or beautiful in everything. You need only look.

MAKE YOUR MARK
Find or create your own idea of beauty. This is especially important if you live or work in an unpleasing place.

APPRECIATE BEAUTY
Natural environments have been altered throughout history. They will only remain unspoiled if they are actively cared for.

82 APPRECIATE THE WHOLE

As your mental horizons expand, you will discover suffering (both great and small) as well as beauty in the world. Acknowledging this is an inevitable part of your greater awareness. Try to view suffering with compassion.

OFFER HELP WHEN IT IS NEEDED
Compassionate action grows naturally from meditation. When the need arises, you might be moved to help in some way.

83 DEALING WITH EVERYDAY SETBACKS

Problems and setbacks are part of life, so try not to hold a fixed view of how things should be. Setbacks can often mean disappointment, but may bring new challenges. Rather than brooding over your altered expectations, accept what comes, and try not to fix the outcome of future events. Your language is an indicator of your attitude. Is a glass half full or half empty? It all depends on your viewpoint. With a new viewpoint, your setbacks might become positive opportunities.

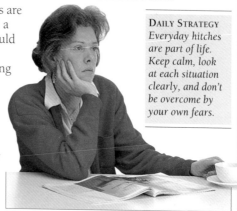

DAILY STRATEGY
Everyday hitches are part of life. Keep calm, look at each situation clearly, and don't be overcome by your own fears.

CHANGE YOUR PERSPECTIVE
Many everyday annoyances and irritations are minor. Do your best to keep them in perspective.

TIME FOR A CHANGE
You may anticipate a change in your life, like retirement, but it can still come as a shock. Take plenty of time to readjust.

84 RESPONDING TO SUDDEN CHANGE

Change can shake the foundations of the life you have created, yet life changes all the time. Remembering this can make it easier to cope with sudden change. When it happens, be aware of how you feel, and recognize that it can be disturbing. Don't hide your feelings: discussing them with people close to you can help you to overcome anxiety, fear, and confusion. Use meditation to keep focused on the present, while letting go of future plans. Sudden change can literally "take your breath away", so stay in touch with your breath to cope with shock.

85 JUST BE KIND

Kindness is a way of putting your new awareness into action by giving something of yourself. It shows that you have noticed what someone else needs, or would like. People do not always ask for what they need in words, so your kindness will involve understanding and relating to others from your heart. Think back to the times in your life when you have been helped by the kindness of others – and what it meant to you. Remember to include yourself as you start practising kindness: it can be all too easy to be hard on yourself.

GOOD OPPORTUNITY
There are always opportunities in life for simple kindnesses.

86 DAILY CHOICES

Every day you have numerous choices to make, which you may not even notice. These are not life-changing decisions, but just minor, day-to-day ones. Each choice brings an opportunity for you to behave, think, react, or respond through self-awareness. However small, your choice has consequences, like ripples in a pond. Try to observe the consequences of your decisions. Do you make the most of every single opportunity?

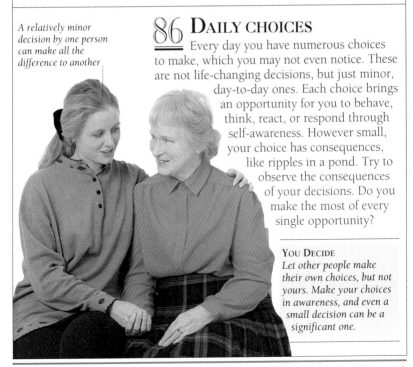

A relatively minor decision by one person can make all the difference to another

YOU DECIDE
Let other people make their own choices, but not yours. Make your choices in awareness, and even a small decision can be a significant one.

87 GREET EACH DAY WITH A SMILE

How you wake up sets the tone for the rest of the day. Do you look forward to the day, or feel weary just thinking of what lies ahead? Note each sensation as you emerge from sleep to become fully awake. Greet the day with a smile and, while still lying in bed, make up your mind to seek opportunities for helping others this day, filling it with kindness. Use this morning exercise to establish a positive attitude that will allow you to make the most of each day.

GET UP & GO
You can meditate while going about your morning routine. As you bathe, think about water and its gift of life.

◁ **A GOOD START**
Exercise, such as a gentle run or some easy stretches, will give you a morning boost of energy.

Focus attention on achieving inner calm

Concentrate on how your body moves and feels

KEEP AN OPEN MIND
When you are ready to begin the day's activities, put aside all preconceptions about the day. Cultivate anticipation and openness to whatever is ahead, and keep the day's events firmly in perspective.

◁ **PREPARE FOR TODAY**
Give yourself ten minutes each and every morning to collect your thoughts quietly. Try to look forward to what the day may bring with feelings of hope and cheerfulness.

This position may be more comfortable if you place a small cushion or soft folded towel between your feet for your buttocks to rest on

88 PREPARING TO REST & SLEEP

Before going to bed, sit quietly and recollect the events of the day, running through them in your mind like a film. You could observe your own participation, or just recall its events, but try not to dwell on any difficulties. If the day has contained struggle or antagonism, avoid recalling entire episodes. This regular practice will enable you to find the sense of perspective and continuity that underpins all aspects of your life. This perspective is particularly valuable if you find it hard to juggle different roles, or the conflicting demands of home, business, and leisure.

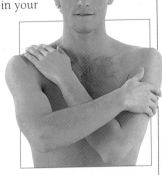

READINESS FOR TOMORROW
To help you sleep, use self-massage to ease any tension in your body, or relax with a warm, non-alcoholic drink.

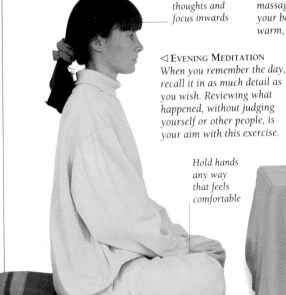

Turn your thoughts and focus inwards

◁ **EVENING MEDITATION**
When you remember the day, recall it in as much detail as you wish. Reviewing what happened, without judging yourself or other people, is your aim with this exercise.

Hold hands any way that feels comfortable

Light from a candle is soft and warm

LIFE CHANGES

89 TOWARDS FULFILMENT

Meditation begins the process of change, as if you have planted a new seed within yourself. Like any seed, it needs nurturing and time to grow. Meditation brings self-awareness to all areas of daily life. As you appreciate your own needs, abilities, and qualities more, you are likely to choose the activities that continue to support your development. Personal fulfilment brings satisfaction and a sense of purpose in life. Imagine sitting beside a pool covered with water-lilies. Some are in bud; some are just opening. Which ones are you?

Yoga pose for meditation: the padmasana or full lotus

◁ **TRANSFORMATION**
Rooted in mud, rising through the water, and blooming under the sun, the flowering of the lotus represents human potential and aspiration.

EASTERN SYMBOL
A lotus bloom means spiritual flowering. Its many petals represent the unfolding of your inner qualities.

90 YOU ARE WHAT YOU EAT

Your choice of food reflects your life values: you will probably eat with more awareness as these values change. What can you learn from the choices you make currently about food? Has your food been produced in a way that is harmful to the environment or to animals? Do you choose over-sugary or fatty food, cigarettes or alcohol that may be harmful to you? Your eating habits may change as you consider the results of each decision you make.

VEGETABLE SALAD WITH
OLIVES & PEPPERS

91 YOU ARE WHAT YOU THINK

Be aware of the power of your mind. It is important to acknowledge the kind of thoughts you have. Consider the saying, "Energy follows thought". Your thoughts predispose you to view everything in a particular way. Habitual thinking creates very strong patterns that can become hard to break. What kind of thoughts fill your mind? Watch your thoughts and discover the patterns they most often fall into. Even long-standing patterns can be changed through awareness.

SWITCHED ON
Stubborn patterns of thinking can mould your life out of shape. Switch on awareness and break the mould.

ENERGY-EFFICIENT?
What kind of energy follows your thought? Being trapped in habitual patterns of negative thinking can make you less productive and less efficient.

92 POSITIVE LIFE CHOICES

Being truly alive involves making fundamental choices. A big decision can be hard when options seem finely balanced. Take your thoughts into a quiet state of meditation, and let your intuition and intellect – rather than your emotions – look at the situation. Use meditation to help you choose positively. Regular meditation may change your goals; let your decisions reflect new hopes.

Decisions arise when priorities change

THINK POSITIVELY
Constructive life choices contribute to your spiritual growth, emotional well-being, and physical energy. Make choices to minimize stress, and create more time to pursue your own interests if you can.

BE CLEAR ABOUT YOUR GOALS

93 ALL LIFE HAS PURPOSE

Human life is just one thread in a much broader tapestry. Animal and plant life interconnect to create a living ecosystem. Human exploitation of animals for profit has led to a great deal of damage. Many spiritual traditions teach compassion and respect for life: all life has its own purpose. Choose an animal and meditate on its life as a living, feeling creature in its own right. Try considering the value even of things you dislike or that appear insignificant to you.

PRESERVE THE BALANCE
This snake may be dangerous, but like all living things it has its part to play in the balance of nature. Today, many species are in danger of becoming extinct.

94 MAKING CONNECTIONS

Meditation helps you find a real sense of connection with the world. Develop this idea by taking the theme of interdependence for your meditation. Sit and reflect upon the many people who invisibly touch your life every day. Like bees in a hive, everyone has something to contribute to the greater whole. Think of the people who are helped directly and indirectly by your own work. Reflect on how others help you in both these ways.

WORLDWIDE NETWORK
Be aware of all the goods that come to you from around the world. Every time you make a cup of tea, eat an orange, or wear cotton or silk, you benefit from this interdependence.

Find connections in the natural world

95 LIVE NOW

Living now is not the same as living for today. It means living fully in each moment of the present, but with a lively awareness of the continuity between past, present, and future. Make time your ally: plant the seeds of your future in the present, through your aspirations. If you wait for tomorrow to start something new, you may never do it. The future is only yours when it has become the present, so try to let every moment of your life be mindful.

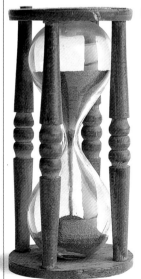

LOSING TIME
Time is constantly running away, so don't let opportunities for compassionate action or simple kindness slip through your fingers.

START TODAY
Avoid letting yourself sit and dream your life away. You have hopes and desires for the future, but don't wait for tomorrow; live life now.

96 EVERY MOMENT COUNTS

You can start to live consciously right this minute. You may not have tomorrow but you do have the present moment. As the saying goes, "Never put off until tomorrow what you can do today". The demon, Mahakala, reminds Buddhists of the passing of time. Who can stand against him? Try not to waste time by dwelling on what is past or trying to imagine your life in the future.

The demon, Mahakala, Power of Devouring Time

MARKING TIME
Do you feel that months and years go by with no real achievement or sense of purpose? Bring your awareness back to living in the present.

Meditate on the passage of time. Live in the present: seize the day

DEVOURING TIME
Here, time is depicted as a monster. Your past, or your future commitments, can easily rule your life, if allowed. See time differently; it affords you many opportunities in the present.

Mahakala shows inevitability and mortality. In his headdress is a flaying knife, and in one hand, a skull cup of blood

97 WELCOME NEW IDEAS

During your journey into meditation, you will encounter many new ideas, some thousands of years old. These have stood the test of time and served generations of seekers well. Judge ideas and values by the kind of people who live their lives by them. Consider what kind of person you wish to become. Be open and receptive to new thoughts and ideas, and other ways of looking at the world.

As technology has greater impact, so you may value human qualities even more

CLEAR SIGHT
View information through insight. Try to develop both intellect and intuition. Read widely, think deeply, and retain your sense of discrimination.

CHANGING TIMES
The practice of meditation has survived centuries of change – and will no doubt last for many more.

98 WHAT'S IMPORTANT TO YOU?

As meditation becomes part of your everyday life, ask yourself if your personal values and aims have become clearer. It is all too easy to be carried along by other people's values and goals. Your regular meditation practice will help you to find out what is really important to you. If you find it hard to identify long-term aspirations, get into the habit of asking yourself what is really significant on a daily basis. This will keep you focused and in touch with your own needs.

99 CHANGE YOURSELF, CHANGE THE WORLD

Meditation produces change. As you change so the world is changed. Although you might think that you personally make little difference to the wider world, when many people think in the same life-affirming way, positive results always take place. Countless people worldwide regularly practise meditation of some kind: you are not alone in your interest, but one of this alliance. At this stage, you may find it both helpful and encouraging to join a class or work with a teacher.

HOW YOU LIVE COULD TIP THE BALANCE

100 SEEING THE BIG PICTURE

Like-minded people join together to express their hope and shared commitment. Create an image of the globe in your mind's eye, and think of the worldwide community of meditators. See the globe held in a network of light. This is the big picture. Meditation brings the light inward, into your life. Mental clarity, insight, and mindful actions illuminate all areas of your daily life and relationships.

MEETING OF MINDS
All types of festivals and celebrations bring people together to mark special events. These gatherings can be an opportunity to share your ideas with others.

101 TOWARDS ENLIGHTENMENT

Enlightenment is an experience that can happen as a result of meditation. It is as if you are suddenly awake. Meditation can create a breakthrough in the way you see everything in your life. This is sometimes a very dramatic moment, like a light going on in your mind. Try not to expect a complete revelation; new ideas and breakthroughs can happen all the time. Every time you discover something new, you bring light into your life. Once you meditate on a regular basis, you will always be moving towards enlightenment.

YOUR JOURNEY TOWARDS ENLIGHTENMENT CAN BE ONE OF SELF-DISCOVERY

INDEX

ACKNOWLEDGMENTS

Dorling Kindersley would like to thank Hilary Bird for compiling the index,
Fiona Wild and Richard Hammond for proof-reading, Jennifer Silkstone
for picture research, and Robert Campbell for DTP assistance.

Photography

KEY: t *top*; b *bottom*; c *centre*; l *left*; r *right*

The publisher would like to thank the following for their kind permission to
reproduce the photographs: AKG, London 22, 52, 66; Ancient Art and
Architecture 8r, 9l; British Museum 68t; Bruce Coleman Limited/Luiz Claudio
Marigo 57b/Kim Taylor 21l, 25; Werner Forman Archive 9r; Fortean Picture
Library 51t; Robert Harding Picture Library 10t, 12r/Westlight/Craig Aurness 13t;
NASA 10c, 51b, 55b; The Image Bank/Joanna McCarthy 30t, b/Kaz Mori 28t;
Museum of the Order of St John/DK 51c; Anne and Bury Peerless Picture
Library 50; Royal College of Music Junior Department 26tr; Tony Stone
Images 32r/Tony Arruza 68b/Warren Bolster 36c/Rob Boudreau 34b/Chad
Ehlers 6b/Ragnar Sigurdsson 38t/Greg Vaughn 54t/Charlie Waite 49b/Ken
Welsh 34t; Zefa Picture Library 33t.

All other photographs by Max Alexander, Steve Bartholomew, Paul Bricknell,
Joe Cornish, Andy Crawford, Tim Daly, Geoff Dann, Jo Foord, Steve Gorton,
Frank Greenaway, Stephen Hayward/Steven Wooster, Colin Keates, Dave King,
Neil Lukas, Andrew McRobb, Ray Moller, David Murray, Stephen Oliver,
Tim Ridley, Kim Sayer, Carl Shone, Jane Stockman, Harry Taylor,
Andreas Von Einsiedel, Matthew Ward, Jerry Young.